We Never Have Time for Just Us...

Wayne Rickerson

Regal Books
A Division of GL Publications
Ventura, CA U.S.A.

Other good reading:
Getting Your Family Together by Wayne Rickerson
How to Help the Christian Home by Wayne Rickerson

The foreign language publishing of all Regal books is under the direction of Gospel Literature International (GLINT). GLINT provides financial and technical help for the adaptation, translation and publishing of books for millions of people worldwide. For information regarding translation contact: GLINT, P.O. Box 6688, Ventura, California 93006.

Published by Regal Books
A Division of GL Publications
Ventura, California 93006
Printed in U.S.A.

Library of Congress Catalog Card No. 81-52941
ISBN 0-8307-0811-1

Contents

INTRODUCTION

A few years ago Janet and I started doing something together that revolutionized our marriage. We started having weekly Husband-Wife Together Times. These weekly "dates" have brought a closeness to our marriage that we never thought possible.

The major purpose of this book is to share how to have weekly Together Times in your marriage. Janet and I feel that any couple who will commit themselves to a once-a-week time together will build a closer, happier marriage.

In addition to showing you how to have a weekly together time we have included 52 Together Time Plans to use during the year.

But this is more than just a book of husband-wife together times. We include six vital steps to husband-wife togetherness. These are: Step 1—A commitment to growth in our marriage; Step 2—A commitment to have weekly Together Times; Step 3—A commitment to be open with each other; Step 4—A commitment to match expectations in our marriage; Step 5—A commitment to accept my spouse; Step 6—A commitment to plan for shared goals and interests, fun and excitement in our marriage.

How to Use This Book

It is obvious by the title of this book that it is to be used by a husband and wife together. In many cases one person will become interested in the book and then share the idea with his/her spouse. Ideally the spouse will respond positively to the book and the idea of husband-wife together times. If this is the case the couple should then read the book a chapter at a time and discuss it. There are questions at the end of each chapter to aid discussion. Answer these separately and then discuss them together.

Now I am well aware that our situations in marriage many times are not ideal. You may share your enthusiasm for together times with your spouse and the response you receive is less than what you would wish. A word of caution in such cases: Do not pressure your spouse if he or she is not yet ready for the steps in this book. Many times within a marriage we are at different stages of personal and spiritual growth. At such times, as difficult as it is, we have to wait until our spouse is prepared for change. Pressuring each other only delays the key things we want accomplished.

If you are in the above situation read the book and answer the questions on your own. The chapters will give insights into your marriage and prepare you for that time when your spouse will be ready for Together Times. When your spouse is ready to join you in this venture of togetherness, once again read the chapters, answer the questions at the end of each chapter, and discuss them with your spouse.

Some of you will be using this book in small groups with other couples. Section 3, "How to Help Couples in Your Church" gives specific guidelines on how to use this book in small groups, Sunday School classes, and at marriage retreats.

I would like to challenge each person who reads this book and puts the principles into action to pass it on. *You can be the key to helping other couples achieve the closeness you are experiencing in your marriage.* Read Section 3 closely and then share with other couples how they can have togetherness in their marriage.

Section I

Six
Vital
Steps
to
Husband-Wife
Togetherness

STEP 1—A COMMITMENT TO GROWTH IN OUR MARRIAGE

It had not been a good year for our marriage—too many moves and problems that were a drain on the emotions. Janet, my wife, was fighting what seemed to be a losing battle with depression. Our poor ways of communicating with each other were putting a dark cloud of gloom over our home. I can remember thinking, "How can this be happening to us? We both want a good marriage, but things are getting worse, not better."

Having done everything I could think of, I was finally ready to listen to God. The message was strong and clear. "Wayne, commit yourself to your marriage and understanding Janet."

"But Lord," I argued, "I am committed to my family. Look how I stress family togetherness. We never miss a family night and I have special times with each of my children. Haven't you read my book *Good Times for Your Family*?".

"But, Wayne, what's that got to do with a commitment to your marriage and understanding Janet? It's easy for you to work on 'your brand' of family togetherness. How about putting first things first for once!"

"OK, Lord, I understand." And I really did. For the first time in our marriage I was ready to do things God's way. I had claimed to put marriage first, but I really hadn't. Before God in prayer I now committed myself to understanding Janet and to growth in our marriage.

I realized that this decision must carry action with it. I decided to suggest something I knew Janet had wanted for a long time. I shared with Janet my new commitment to our marriage. She looked hopeful. But when I suggested a weekly together time to communicate, plan, read the Bible and pray together, she was enthusiastic. "I think that would be great! When do we start?"

We have been having these weekly times together for more than six years now. I really believe that this has been the most significant step we have ever taken for growth in our marriage.

Janet puts it like this, "Wayne's suggestion for a weekly time together was a real turnaround for our marriage. We both started working hard at getting rid of the old hurtful ways of communicating. Together time brought us together in a single purpose—to understand each other better and improve our marriage. Now I can't imagine our marriage without together times."

I couldn't agree more. Working on our schedules, discussing family matters, sharing, reading and discussing Scripture and praying together on a regular basis has brought a real sense of oneness to our relationship. It is a tool for continued growth in marriage. A tool we want to share with you in this manual.

COMMITMENT—Foundation for Growth in Marriage

I have found that there are two kinds of commitment essential to a growing marriage: First is a personal commitment to God through faith in Jesus Christ; next is a commitment to our marriage. These comprise the firm foundation from which we can have solid growth in our marriage.

Our personal commitment to God leads us to want our marriage to be all that He desires. God wants us to give our marriage top billing, as He so carefully tells us in His Word:

"Then the Lord God said, 'It is not good for the man to be alone; I will make him a helper suitable for him.' And out of the ground the Lord God formed every beast of the field and every bird of the sky, and brought them to the man to see what he would call them; and whatever the man called a living creature, that was its name. And the man gave names to all the cattle, and to the birds of the sky, and to every beast of the field, but for Adam there was not found a helper suitable for him. So the Lord God caused a deep sleep to fall upon the man, and he slept; then He took one of his ribs, and closed up the flesh at that place. And the Lord God fashioned into a woman the rib which He had taken from the man, and brought her to the man. And the man said, 'This is now bone of my bones, and flesh of my flesh; she shall be called Woman, because she was taken out of Man.' For this cause a man shall leave his father and his mother, and shall cleave to his wife; and they shall become one flesh. And the man and his wife were both naked and were not ashamed" (Gen. 2:18-25).

Notice several important thoughts about this passage. First is that marriage is ordained by God. It is the first human institution. The first human relationship is husband and wife. God, throughout His Word, gives the husband-wife relationship top priority.

Verse 24 is very important for us to understand, for it is God's first instruction on how husband and wife are to relate. First man is to "leave" his father and mother. The emphasis here is upon untying one relationship before tying another. Now the husband and wife's responsibility is primarily their marriage relationship—described now as a cleaving to each another.

"Cleave" means to weld, grip or adhere together. When a man "cleaves" to his wife, they become *one flesh*. The term "one flesh" is a beautiful capsule description of the oneness, completeness and permanence God intended in the marriage relationship. "One flesh" suggests a unique oneness—a total commitment to intimacy in all of life together, symbolized by sexual union."[1]

While in one sense we are already "one flesh" in marriage, there is another sense in which we become "one flesh" by working toward intimacy in our marriage relationship. Intimacy in marriage means committing ourselves to understanding and accepting our spouse.

Intimacy also means sharing with our spouse who we really are: our deepest feelings of fears, frustrations, hurts, and joys. This does involve some risk yet a necessary risk. As Paul Tournier puts it, "A complete unveiling of one's inner thoughts, an absolute necessity for real and deep understanding, demands a great deal of courage."[2] But courage to unveil our innermost thoughts opens the door to intimacy in marriage.

ACTION—Result of Commitment

The kind of commitment I have been talking about requires action. I knew when I told Janet I was committing myself to growth in our marriage that I must do something specific.

This was a new thought to me. For years I thought marriage was something that would just grow naturally. I've found since that many persons have this same misconception. But I now know that anything worth achieving takes planning and effort. Marriage is no exception.

I like the way Paul Tournier, the great Christian physician and psychotherapist, puts it. "What really counts, then, is the working out together of marital happiness. It is a goal to strive after, not a privilege gained at the outset. And to work it out, the ability to understand each other is essential."[3]

In this manual I suggest one step of action you can take to assist you in the "working out of marital happiness." If you will commit yourself to having together times, I feel that your marriage will grow. It is my feeling that couples should have a "date" each week to concentrate on their marriage. A time all to themselves. I have seen great things happen in marriages where couples commit themselves to together times. In Step 2 I explain how these together times work.

Questions to Answer and Discuss

1. Who has influenced your attitudes toward marriage and in what ways have these attitudes been influenced?

2. In what ways do you feel that a personal commitment to God affects a marriage relationship?

3. What are some things that prevent couples from giving their marriage "top billing"?

4. The author states that you must "untie" one relationship (family) before "tying" another (marriage). What problems have you encountered doing this? How has it affected your marriage?

5. What implications does the word "cleave" have for your marriage?

6. The author states that there is a sense in which we become "one flesh" by working toward intimacy in marriage. What do you feel intimacy in marriage means? Use specific examples.

7. Paul Tournier says that "a complete unveiling of one's inner thoughts, an absolute necessity for real and deep understanding, demands a great deal of courage." Do you agree or disagree with this statement? Why?

8. Finish the statement, "Commitment in marriage to me means —————————————————————— .

9. After reflecting on the above questions, I have discovered the following about my commitment to my marriage:

10. Because of these insights I will make the following changes within myself to enrich our marriage:

If you are studying this book in a small-group session: Summarize insights you have gained into better understanding your spouse.

Sometime before your next group session: Share answers 9 and 10 with your spouse. Also share your summary of insights.

STEP 2—A COMMITMENT TO HAVE WEEKLY TOGETHER TIMES

Barbara was thrilled. "I'll never forget how special I felt," she said, "when Skip told the vice-president of the University of Portland that he wouldn't be able to make the meeting because he had a date with his wife for our together time."

I smiled as I envisioned the look on that vice-president's face when Major Skip Centioli, an instructor in the University's R.O.T.C. program, turned down the meeting *for a date with his wife.*

I can imagine his thoughts went something like this: "What's happened to Major Centioli? He must be losing his marbles. He used to be such a reliable officer—so committed to his job. Since when does a wife come before a man's job?"

Skip's wife did not always come before his job. For many years it was work first. Skip and Barb assumed, like

Janet and I did, that the marriage would take care of itself. When it didn't, Skip and Barb decided to commit themselves to a growing marriage. I can remember so vividly two years ago when they made that commitment. Janet and I led 25 other couples in our annual marriage enrichment retreat. We shared the concept of commitment to a growing marriage. We had each couple share in Husband-Wife Together Time.

On that weekend Skip committed his life to the Lord and his marriage to growth. In the two years since the retreat, I have been astounded at what that commitment has done for the Centioli family. One of Skip and Barb's first steps of action was to start a regular together time.

"This time," Skip recently told me, "has allowed us to get below the superficial levels of conversation. During this time we have been able to express our goals, frustrations, concerns and joys."

For Barb, together times have brought a new freshness to the marriage. "I have become a happier and more satisfied wife since we started having together times. I have become more aware of Skip's needs and his schedule, the pressure he is under at work, and I'm beginning to understand he has feelings too!"

Many family specialists feel that such husband-wife "dates" are important if a couple wants to have a growing marriage. One such specialist, Dennis Guernsey in his book *Thoroughly Married,* considers quality husband-wife together time indispensable for meaningful communication in marriage. Dr. Guernsey, speaking of this meaningful communication, says, "First it requires learning how to spend time with each other in meaningful interaction and conversation. It is a skill and not something that just 'happens.' It requires deliberately setting aside a time to be with each other—time that is regular, in the sense of being dependable."[4]

How to Have Husband-Wife Together Times

I would like to share with you a plan that you and your spouse can use to draw closer together. True, it will take commitment. You will need to set aside an hour a week. It is a simple plan—a workable plan that I have shared with hundreds of other couples.

First, decide together if Husband-Wife Together Time is something you are willing to commit yourselves to. *It is important not to push each other into this.* Some spouses may want more time to think about this commitment.

Decide on a time that is dependable. For a couple of years Janet and I had our together times at 8:30 as soon as the children were in bed. We now have it at noon because I am able to come home for lunch and the children are in school. Some couples might be able to have the same night each week. For others this will not be possible. Janet and I choose a time at the first of the week when we can meet. A word of warning here. You will never just *have* time for this. You must *make* time! Together time must be moved to the top of your list of priorities. *Don't let anything interfere with your date.*

Find a quiet place where you will not be interrupted. Skip and Barb have their together time tucked away in a quiet corner of a restaurant. Janet and I prefer our family room table.

You will notice that there are 52 together-time guides. These are not meant to be inflexible plans from which you dare not depart. They are simply guides. Somewhere to start. Feel free to come up with your own format—something you're comfortable with. Remember, it is not the method that counts. What is important is that you have some kind of meaningful interaction each week.

Here is how each plan works: One of you should read aloud the quote at the top of the together time. This gives the theme of your time together. The discussion questions and Scripture that follow are all related to the theme. Under each of these there is space to write down your thoughts. This will help you put into practice insights you have gained. It will also give you something to look back on and see how your marriage has grown. Next, there are four things for you to do together:

1. *Let's Talk.* Each "Let's Talk" section suggests a couple of discussion questions relating to the theme. You may discuss one of these, both, or choose your own topic of discussion. Decide together what to discuss.

A word of caution here. Don't pressure each other to talk about something one of you does not feel ready for yet. For many, sharing feelings is a new experience. Often a person needs to start with light communication and move gradually to deeper levels of sharing feelings.

Many times Janet and I have jotted down things during the week that we want to discuss during our together time. In some instances we save the "heavies"—problems that are quite emotional—for this time. As Janet says, "I feel very secure in knowing I can bring up anything at this time and we will discuss it in a reasonable manner."

Don't, however, make this a time when you bring your list of weekly complaints. Share your feelings in as positive and non-threatening way as possible. Steps three and five, "A Commitment to Be Open with My Spouse" and "A Commitment to Accept My Spouse," will give you insights on how to communicate feelings in a positive way.

Remember, your goal is always to first, understand your spouse and secondly, to be understood.

2. *Let's Plan.* Janet is most enthusiastic about this "Let's Plan" part of our together time. "Working out our schedules on our planning calendar is very important to

me," she says. "We used to have so many conflicts just because we didn't let each other know what we were doing during the week. Now we have almost eliminated this kind of conflict."

Use monthly planning calendars to work out your schedules. You will be able to see when you are getting overscheduled. Always ask, "Are we allowing enough family time?" This is a good time to plan family activities such as Family Night.

3. *Let's Read God's Word.* This time of reading God's Word and praying together with Janet is very important to me. I feel a special closeness to her as we read and discuss God's Word together and then pray for each other and for other concerns.

These times can bind couples together in a very special way. I agree with Dr. Tournier that sharing spiritual matters "is the highest tie binding a couple together and yet it is so rare."

We suggest that each week you alternate the responsibility for reading the suggested passage of Scripture. You and your spouse should then share what the Scripture says to you and how these insights apply to your marriage and family. Remember that this is a time of sharing—not one person teaching the other. This is simply reading God's Word together and sharing your personal thoughts and feelings. Each of you has a personal relationship with God that can be helpful when shared with the other.

4. *Let's Pray.* First Janet and I make a list of things to pray about—the children, our marriage and things for which we are thankful. We share in a time of prayer. I can't begin to explain how much it means to me to hear Janet thank God for my contribution to our family and pray for my efforts in our home.

And so ends our weekly together time. But each end-ing is really a new beginning for our relationship to each other.

I have now shared with you how to have husband and wife together time. But let me emphasize once again that this is only a guide. Please feel free to use it any way you wish. The format is not the important thing. What is important, however, is to have a regular, quality time together.

The Together Time guides can be used in a variety of ways.

Questions to Answer and Discuss

1. First read Step 2. Next have a together time. After completing your together time answer the following questions.

2. How did you feel about your together time? Circle one or more: Nervous   at ease   pleased   elated together   pressured

3. What part of the together time was most helpful to you?

4. What part of the together time was most difficult for you?

5. How did you feel during the Scripture and prayer time?

6. What effect do you feel regular together times could have on your marriage?

7. When you think of committing yourself to regular together times, how do you feel?

8. What do you feel will be your greatest stumbling block to having regular together times?

9. After reflecting on the above questions, I have discovered the following about myself:

10. Because of these insights, I will make the following changes within myself to enrich our marriage:

If you are studying this book in a small-group session: Summarize insights you have gained into better understanding your spouse.

Sometime before your next group session: Share answers 9 and 10 with your spouse. Also share your summary of insights.

STEP 3—A COMMITMENT TO BE OPEN WITH EACH OTHER

I was afraid, angry and disappointed. I wondered where God was. I wondered where I was. But I was alone with my thoughts, for you see, men do not share such "weaknesses" with others, especially with their wives.

Janet, interpreting my silence and apparent nonchalance about a sticky family problem as not caring, confronted me. "Wayne, are you going to do something about our financial situation?"

It was like a dam burst. All the emotions I had stored up for the last year flowed out. I sobbed as I admitted my fears, feelings of failure of not being able to handle family matters. I really felt I'd blown it. Now Janet would feel insecure because she would know that I didn't have things under control. I waited for the family walls to come crumbling down.

But they didn't. Just the opposite happened. Instead of falling apart Janet seemed very relieved. "You do have feelings!" she said. "Sometimes I wondered. It's not knowing what you were feeling that was frustrating to me. Now I feel we can face this problem together."

This encounter was a valuable lesson to me. I learned that sharing my feelings was not a sign of weakness but actually a sign of strength. It was a relief to know that I didn't have to wear the "mask of manliness" that I had learned to wear so masterfully. This experience led me, slowly I will admit, to a new openness with Janet and others. The benefits are a growing closeness in our marriage through mutual openness—the sharing of feelings.

Mask of Manliness

I have noticed that I am not the only one who wears a mask of manliness. Most of us men do. We wear that mask partly because we have been asked to by society. "Boys don't cry"; "Be a man"; "Be strong." All of which says, "Keep your feelings inside; exposing such monsters is a sign of weakness."

But we men also wear a mask of manliness because we want to. It's so available. Easy to put on. It's comfortable and safe. So we hide our feelings from others and *from ourselves*, for as John Powell says, "I can only know that much of myself which I have the courage to confide in you."

Men, I am convinced that it is extremely important that we take off our masks and learn to express and hear feelings. If we are not in tune with our own feelings, then we certainly will not be in tune with our wives' feelings and intimacy in marriage; oneness will never happen.

I'm not sure what his name was, but Janet and I called him "Mountain Man." He was massive, at least six-feet-four and weighed about 260 pounds with bushy hair and matching beard. He looked like he should have been playing tackle for the L.A. Rams rather than attending a Marriage Encounter weekend, a two-day session on how to communicate feelings in marriage. But there he was, and when we were asked to share how we felt about the weekend the "Mountain Man" said, "I don't know how my wife got me here (I had wondered that myself) but now we are closer than we have been in years."

It was obvious to me from the man's brusque mannerism that he had worn his mask with pride. But in two days he had learned what being open in marriage was all about. He had taken off his mask and, as he said, it had brought a new closeness to his marriage.

Up to this point it might seem that I have laid the responsibility for openness in marriage wholly upon the shoulders of the male, but not so. A reluctance to be open and share feelings is a problem with women as well as men; really a human problem. All of us, to some extent, have masks we hide behind that need to come off. We hide behind these because there is risk involved in being open. We become vulnerable. The risk we take may mean rejection. By being open we may stir up feelings of inadequacy or fear or old hurts. But whatever the risk, it is worth it; for each of us needs the kind of intimacy that open communication brings. We each have a deep human need, placed there by God, to be close to someone. In marriage God has given us a mate that can provide us with the deepest closeness and understanding. To have this closeness *both husband and wife must commit themselves to openness in marriage.*

Learning to Be Open

Over the last several years Janet and I have learned some basic principles of sharing feelings that have helped us to become more open. I'd like to share these with you now.

1. *We all have the same basic range of feelings.* Feelings are sensations that can either give us pleasure or

pain. These feelings can be caused by thoughts or by reactions to certain circumstances. For example, a loud noise can give me a feeling of fear. A wife can feel angry when her husband is continually late for dinner. Her thoughts that trigger the feeling might be, "If he really cared about me he would be on time or phone."

Our feelings range from negative, such as anger, fear, frustration, rejection, tiredness, tension, panic, nervousness, dependency, to the positive, such as being loving, calm, relaxed, happy, pleased, excited, proud, creative, close, loving and appealing.

Our differences come in the intensity of these feelings and the way we express them.

2. *These feelings are neither good nor bad.* Feelings are just there. What we *do* with our feelings can be good or bad. Jesus, the God-man, had our full range of human emotions, but He was sinless. For example, when Jesus experienced fear in the Garden of Gethsemane He did not run but faced His responsibility. He, at times, was angry but did not sin.

3. *We must be able to accept the other person's feelings.* I'll have to admit that I had trouble with this one for a long time. I can remember arguing with my wife about her feelings. "That's ridiculous!" I would say. "You shouldn't be feeling that way," or even try to convince her that she wasn't feeling that way. But she *was* feeling that way and there was nothing I could say that would change that.

To accept another's feelings does not mean that we have to agree that he or she "should" feel that way, or that the feelings are "right" or "wrong." Acceptance *does mean* that we should give that person a right to his or her own feelings; acknowledge that he or she is indeed experiencing those feelings, and try to the best of our abilities to understand them.

4. *We must own our own feelings.* This is a critical area in communicating our feelings to our spouse. If you say, "You make me so mad when you spend time with everyone but me," two things happen. First you eliminate any chance of your spouse hearing your real feelings because he has reacted to the first thing you said, "you." Now he is getting ready to defend himself, not get in tune with your feelings. You have accused your spouse of "making" you feel a certain way. For sure he has contributed to the circumstances that produced that feeling, but he has not crawled inside you and forced you to feel that way. It is your feeling and it should be expressed that way. For example, the frustration mentioned above could have been stated, "I feel angry and rejected when I see you spending more time with other people than with me." In this case you have owned your feeling by saying "I feel" and your chances for being understood are much greater.

5. *We must practice listening to feelings—our own and our spouse's—and expressing feelings if we want to achieve intimacy in marriage!*

Start becoming conscious of how you are feeling—not just thinking—by making "I" statements: "I feel hurt when you do that," not "You hurt me when you do that." Become conscious of how your spouse is feeling. Identify with your spouse's feelings by saying, "You seem to be feeling . . ." (anxious, happy, frustrated, etc.). Remember to accept your spouse's feelings.

Together Times are a good time to practice listening and expressing feelings. Some of the discussion questions are feeling questions. This is a "low risk" time to express feelings because of the positive nature of your time together. You will be rewarded by your commitment to openness in your marriage by a new sense of closeness and understanding.

Questions to Answer and Discuss

1. When you were growing up, what did you learn about your role as a male or female? Have any of these things become "masks" that affect your marriage?

2. The author states that feelings are neither good nor bad. How do you feel about that statement?

3. Write down at least five feelings you have experienced during the last week. Write these in sentence form starting each sentence with "I feel" or "I felt."

4. Why do many of us have a hard time accepting one another's feelings?

5. On a scale of 1-10 rate your ability to "own" your own feelings. (10 is the highest degree of ownership.)

6. Share a time when you felt your feelings were not accepted.

7. Finish the sentence, "I have a hard time accepting another's feelings when I _____ ."

8. For me, the hardest thing about sharing feelings is.

9. After reflecting on the above questions, I have found out the following about how I handle feelings:

10. Because of these insights, I will make the following changes within myself to enrich our marriage:

If you are studying this book in a small-group session: Summarize insights you have gained into better understanding your spouse.

Sometime before your next group session: Share answers 9 and 10 with your spouse. Also share your summary of insights.

STEP 4—A COMMITMENT TO MATCH EXPECTATIONS IN OUR MARRIAGE

It is amazing how many expectations we bring with us into marriage. Some refer to these as our "marriage script"—a mental picture of what we expect our marriage to be like.

We develop this picture in several ways. Some of our expectations are shaped by society. For example, the traditional roles of the husband and wife are being challenged by many today. A man or woman can go into marriage highly influenced by what society is saying about what it means to be a "husband" or a "wife." Expectations can be manipulated by movies, books, magazines and television.

We also have personal needs that shape our expectations of marriage. Some very unhappy persons have gone into marriage hoping that marriage would solve their problems. Because of this unrealistic expectation, they put demands on their spouse.

The biggest influence on our expectations, however,

is what we observed in our parents' marriage. We grew up with that marriage. Even if we felt our parents had a poor marriage, it still shapes many of our assumptions about husband and wife relationships.

Janet and I can certainly see how our parents' marriages have influenced our expectations for our marriage. One expectation that Janet brought into our marriage was that the husband should be a handyman, able to handle all household repairs, maintenance, and building projects. In Janet's home her father did all the repairing, building and such things that needed to be done around the home. Her mother managed the typical household duties. As a result, Janet expected me to carry out my role as Mr. Fixit and Mr. Buildit. Little did she know what was in store for her, for you see, in my home we had a different situation. If my father ever fixed anything it was purely by accident. The happiest day of Dad's life was when he fixed the electric clock on Mom's stove. He took it apart and couldn't find what was wrong. But when he put the clock back together it worked!

Things seldom worked that well for Dad. He would try to fix something, getting more frustrated by the moment until he would finally explode, shouting his favorite four-letter word at the object of his wrath, "Dumb!" I guess that's why he finally developed his philosophy, "If you wait long enough maybe it will fix itself."

I either learned or inherited my father's mechanical inaptitude. I am thoroughly intimidated by anything that takes the slightest bit of mechanical aptitude. I avoid repairing and building things. On those rare occasions when I temporarily lose my sanity and attempt to repair something, our children hide under their beds and my wife discovers suddenly that she needs to go shopping.

As you can see, the stage is set for real conflict in our marriage. We have mismatched expectations. Janet expects little projects to be done around the house—I expect to conveniently overlook them or wait until they complete themselves. Each time Janet walks through a room in the house and sees the uncompleted project, she thinks, "That would only take five minutes. He knows how I feel about this. I resent his lack of concern for my feelings."

Satisfying Expectations

Since unmet expectations cause such resentment it is essential that couples work toward matching their spouse's expectations. Seeds of resentment, even the small unmet expectations, have a way of growing and can crowd out the good things in marriage.

I'd like you to take a moment and list some of the expectations you have for your marriage that are not being met.

1.
2.
3.
4.

Put a check by the ones that cause you the most disappointment.

Now that you have isolated some unmet expectations that are important to you, the next goal is to "match" these expectations with those of your spouse. By "matching" I do not mean that each of your expectations must be met and that each of your spouse's expectations must be met. That, of course, is impossible. What I mean by "match" is a process of evaluating our own expectations, understanding our spouse's expectations, changing that which is reasonable to change and accepting that which will not or cannot be changed. The following three-step experience will help you match expectations in your marriage.

First, evaluate your expectations. Both you and your spouse should take the most important expectation on your list and ask yourself some questions: "Why do I hold this expectation?" "Why is this expectation so important to me?" "Is this a reasonable expectation?" "Is my spouse really capable of meeting this expectation?"

Second, understand your spouse's expectations. After you have taken a close look at yourself, it is now time to share that expectation with your spouse. You might start by saying something like this, "I have an unmet expectation that I would like to share with you. I expect . . ."

It is important not to accuse or blame. Remember to own your own feelings. Share your unmet expectation and the feelings you have when it is not met.

The spouse who is listening to this unmet expectation is to work toward understanding. This is a tall order for most of us. Our natural response is to defend ourselves, become angry, tell the other person his or her expectation is unreasonable, or quickly change the focus and accuse the other person of not meeting our own expectations. Resist that temptation! Listen to the feelings (Remember Step 3?). Try to put yourself in your spouse's place. Ask questions. See if you can restate your spouse's point of view by saying the following. "I hear you saying that you feel '_____.' Is that what you mean?"

When one person has shared an expectation and it has been fully explored, the other person shares an expectation using the same procedure.

Third, change and accept. Through the communication process you have just experienced, you will be brought naturally to this final step. You each need to ask yourself the questions, "Is there something I need to accept? Is there something I need to change?"

When Janet and I used the above process, we were able to resolve our mismatched expectations—projects calling for handyman skills around the house. I shared with her some of my feelings of fear, inadequacy and embarrassment when I tried to become a "handyman."

"I thought you just didn't want to do those things— just didn't care enough about my feelings," she replied when I really leveled. "I really had no idea that was such a difficult area for you to deal with."

Now Janet has accepted my limitations and no longer expects as much from me as a handyman. The jobs, however, still have to be done. We decide together what is the best approach. Is it something I want to take on? Can Janet do the job? Do we need to hire someone to do it?

By changing her attitude Janet has turned situations, that under the old "mismatched" system would have produced conflict, into good experiences for both of us— like the night last year when we bought a stereo and cabinet for the family to enjoy during the Christmas season. At about 9:00 P.M. when the children were in bed we quietly brought our new purchase into the family room to assemble it. I tucked the girls in and when I returned to the family room my heart skipped at least 10 beats. What I saw was a complete disaster. My wife had laid out the pieces of that "easy to assemble" stereo cabinet and it looked like there were at least a thousand pieces. Those old feelings of anxiety started swelling inside me until I realized that my wife was not expecting me to take charge of the assembly. There she was with the directions, carefully laying out the parts.

"This will take us all night," I complained.

"I don't think it is as difficult as it looks," Janet replied. "If you'll just give me a hand we can get it done in an hour or so."

Janet was right. With her leadership the project was finished almost hassle free.

Afterwards we sat back talking about our victory. "You know," Janet said, "when I opened that box and saw all those parts I thought, 'Wayne is going to fall apart. We might as well box it back up and take it to the store.' But then I thought, 'Why? I can follow instructions much better than he. I'll take the lead and we'll be able to get the job done.' "

Do you see what happened? There was understanding of each other's feelings. This led to acceptance and a change in expectations. It turned a potentially bad situation into an enjoyable one. We felt really good about working together.

Sometimes to match expectations, someone needs to change. I counseled one couple where much of the wife's resentment was about the lack of time her husband spent with the family. "He spends most of his time at work and when he does have leisure time he spends it on himself, playing ball or fishing."

The husband agreed. This was a weakness with him. He agreed to change and limit the amount of time on the job and include his family in his leisure time. The expectations were matched.

Sometimes to match expectations there must be a balance of acceptance and change.

Bill and Sharon came into my office to talk to me about their mismatched expectations. "I come home from work and Sharon many times doesn't even acknowledge I'm home. I'd like for her to give me a hug and a kiss and act like she's glad I'm home."

Bill had been raised in a family that expressed love by a lot of physical contact—hugging, kissing, touching. They also said, "I love you" a lot. Sharon, on the other hand, came from a home that did not express love by touching at all. And they seldom said, "I love you" to one another.

Bill expected love to be expressed in the way he had learned it in his home. Sharon did not see the need for it. Mismatched expectations! Sharon came to see that she needed to do some changing. She worked at meeting Bill at the door and express love to him when he arrived home from work. Bill had to realize that he and Sharon had different ways of expressing love and that he could not expect her to be as responsive as was his own family. With this combination of acceptance and change, Bill and Sharon were able to "match" their expectations.

Expectations can be matched. But remember that no marriage can meet all your needs. A happy marriage is one where most of the needs are met most of the time. This can happen through the process of evaluation, understanding and acceptance.

Acceptance is a crucial part of marriage. I have devoted the next step to helping couples develop skills in accepting each other in marriage.

Questions to Answer and Discuss
1. Make a list of expectations you brought into your marriage.

2. Evaluate your list of expectations. Place an *S* by each expectation that has been influenced by society, an *N* by each expectation that is shaped by a personal need and a *P* by each expectation that is a result of your parents' influence.

3. The author states, "Since unmet expectations cause resentment it is essential that couples work toward matching their expectations." React to the author's statement. How important do you feel it is for couples to work toward matching expectations?

4. Take one of the above expectations and share briefly how it has affected your marriage.

5. The author gives a three-step process for matching expectations. Give the strengths or weaknesses you see in this process.

6. What would be most helpful to you in understanding your spouse's expectations?

7. Finish the following sentence. "When an expectation in marriage is not met I feel . . .

8. The author states that "a happy marriage is one where most of the needs are met most of the time." How do you feel about that statement?

9.,10. Together with your spouse, work through the three-step process the author gives for matching expectations in marriage.

If you are studying this book in a small-group session: Summarize insights you have gained into better understanding your spouse.

Sometime before your next group session: Share answers 9 and 10 with your spouse.

STEP 5—A COMMITMENT TO ACCEPT MY SPOUSE

"I just don't understand how you can say that!" I replied to Janet in an angry voice. "I think they do pretty well helping around the house. After all, they're just kids."

This dialogue between Janet and me has taken place many times over the years. I become very frustrated when we discuss this area of family life. Janet is just as frustrated. We just think differently about this area. In the past, I have tried to show Janet where she was "wrong" and tried to help her thinking in this area. It hasn't worked. Now, I've found a better way. I am starting to acknowledge that Janet and I think differently about various things, and that is OK. Janet and I have both come to realize that when we say, "I just can't understand you," what we are really saying is, "I just won't admit that you are different than I am." We now work at not only understanding the other's point of view but also at *being understanding*, which carries with it acceptance of the other person as he is.

Real growth in marriage, Together Times or not, will never happen until we grow in the area of accepting each other. This is a crucial part of understanding in marriage.

The Three Rs of Marriage

To grow in the area of acceptance of one another, it is helpful to see how the problem of nonacceptance creeps into our marriages. There are three stages which most marriages go through which I call the "Three Rs of Marriage."

First, the romantic stage. I'm sure you remember this stage well. Mr. or Ms. "Right" walks into your life. You have all those strong love feelings, and you have so much in common. In fact, you find it amazing how much you think alike in so many areas. The differences? There are some but these are delightful. "I have found a person who complements my personality. This romance," you conclude, "was surely made in heaven."

And well it might be, but in stage two you may, at times, wonder whether it was made in the other place!

Second, the reality stage. The romantic stage does not last forever. Slowly, it phases out as the reality stage comes in. You begin noticing that you really do have some differences. Some of these are just little irritating things, like your spouse not picking up after himself, or not being ready to go places on time, or continually interrupting you while you are trying to read the newspaper or a book.

Some things are more major. You knew that your spouse had a quiet personality when you married her. You liked that because it complemented your more outgoing nature. You certainly didn't want to marry someone as talkative and active as you. Too much competition, you know. But now that same quality you used to admire in your spouse is becoming very irritating. No, irritating is not the word. Maddening is more like it. You would like to go to a party or invite friends over but look who would rather stay home and read a book or work around the house.

The *reality* of your marriage suddenly hits you. You are married to a person very different from yourself. The thought creeps into your mind: "Maybe, just maybe, I have married the wrong person. It could be possible," you think, "that I am not really compatible with this irritating person!"

You are not really happy with the way your marriage is going. You think through your options. "I could try and *'remake'* my spouse. Yes, that is what I will do. I could definitely help my spouse to become a better person. I can see all his (her) faults. I know what can make him (her) into a real lovable person if he (she) would just change!"

So you try this. But an interesting thing happens. The more you try to change your spouse the more he or she resists you and does the things that irritate you. The more irritated you become, the more you try to change your spouse. You finally come to the startling realization that "that stubborn person just isn't going to change."

What now? You are now ready for stage three of your marriage, which offers you some options.

Third, the re-create stage. In this stage you actually think through several options. "I can resign myself to the fact that that's the way he (she) is but I'll resent it. I want more out of our marriage, a real closeness. Or if things are really intolerable I can resign myself from the whole thing and find someone with whom I am really 'compatible.' "

The final option, I believe the Christian choice, is, "I can take personal responsibility to 're-create' or give new life to my marriage. I can change myself and accept my spouse the way he (she) is. For it is only through changing myself, and by accepting my spouse, that changes will occur."

I mentioned earlier Janet's and my disagreements over the children. To re-create our marriage we both had to change our own attitudes toward each other. It was a big step for me to accept Janet's right to her point of view toward the children. It was just as big a step for Janet to accept mine. We still don't agree, but we accept the other's right to be who he or she is. It is much easier for us to work out compromises about the children when we accept each other.

Self-acceptance, however, is a crucial part of accepting others. Before we can really accept our spouse we must be able to accept ourselves. Marriage is vastly improved by a healthy sense of self-esteem. Dr. Bruce Narramore emphasizes the importance of self-acceptance in marriage in his excellent book *You're Something Special.*

"Marriage is another realm where self-acceptance plays an important part. When we don't value ourselves and our abilities, we are likely to be extremely sensitive and edgy. We interpret the slightest suggestion from our mate as harsh criticism, unwanted pressure, or persistent nagging. Whenever a difference of opinion crops up, we struggle to prove our point and defend our position in order to protect our shaky self-esteem."[5]

Janet and I have seen a direct correlation between our own self-acceptance and the acceptance of each other. As I accept who I am, I can accept who she is with her differences—and not be threatened.

That we should value ourselves—have a healthy sense of self-esteem—is deeply rooted in Scripture. In Genesis we are said to have been created in the image of

God (*see* Gen. 1:26). Think of that. Within us we have something of the character of God. What is important is that God accepts us *as we are* when we are His reborn children. God valued me so much that He gave His Son for me. And God would not waste His Son on someone who was not worthwhile!

When we really realize that God values us and accepts us as we are, we become free to become all He wants us to become. And, at the same time, we are able to accept other persons as they are and help free them to achieve their true potentials. Nowhere is this more true than in our marriages.

During your Together Times, accept your spouse's right to be different and think differently. Work toward understanding his or her point of view.

If self-esteem is a sticky problem in your marriage, I suggest you and your spouse read Dr. Narramore's book *You're Something Special*. A commitment to accept yourself and your spouse should be an integral part of your commitment to have a growing marriage.

Questions to Answer and Discuss

1. What experiences in your life have helped make it easy or difficult for you to accept yourself?

2. On a scale of 1-10 rate to what degree you accept yourself (10 is the highest rating for self-esteem).

3. Share briefly how the three stages of marriage—*romantic, reality,* and *re-creation*—have affected how you accept your spouse. At what stage are you now?

4. What effect do you feel your own self-acceptance has on how you accept your spouse?

5. Have you ever experienced a real freedom to change when someone accepted you as you were? Explain.

6. In what area of your life would you most like to be accepted as you are?

7. Finish the sentence, "When I am accepted I feel ＿

8. When we realize that within us is something of the character of God and that as His reborn children we are accepted as we are, what effect can this have on our marriage?

9. After reflecting on the above questions, I have discovered that my ability to accept myself or my spouse is affecting our marriage in the following ways:

10. Because of these insights, I will make the following changes within myself to enrich our marriage:

If you are studying this book in a small-group session: Summarize insights you have gained into better understanding your spouse.

Sometime before your next group session: Share answers 9 and 10 with your spouse. Also share your summary of insights.

STEP 6—A COMMITMENT TO PLAN FOR SHARED GOALS AND INTERESTS, FUN AND EXCITEMENT IN OUR MARRIAGE

Redbook magazine recently asked 730 marriage counselors about the most common problems that pull couples apart. As a result of this survey, *Redbook* found the ten most common marital problems and listed them in the order of frequency:

1. A breakdown in communication
2. The loss of shared goals or interests
3. Sexual incompatibility
4. Infidelity
5. The excitement and fun has gone out of marriage
6. Money
7. Conflicts about children
8. Alcohol and drug abuse
9. Women's equality issues
10. In-laws

Are you surprised at how some of these problems are ranked? I would have guessed that number one would be communication, but numbers 2 and 5 caught me by surprise. Who would think that "The loss of shared goals or interests" and "The excitement and fun has gone out of marriage" would rank so high?

After thinking about numbers 2 and 5 for a while, I realized that their high ranking should not have surprised me for several reasons. First, we are in the "me" decade. Bookstores are full of self-help books and pop psychology books about looking out for "number one." The *focus becomes on the individual* and not the marriage relationship. How can there be shared goals and interests if persons are preoccupied with self-fulfillment? This kind of thinking will, of course, lead to the decline of fun, excitement, and shared goals and interests in marriage.

Another contributing factor is that *many expect too much of marriage.* There is no way that marriage can constantly be fun and exciting as it was in courtship and honeymoon phases. One must be prepared for a certain amount of day-in, day-out routine and, with that, certainly some boredom.

A third factor, and one I feel that every couple is capable of remedying, *is neglect.* We do not go into marriage thinking, "Now our plan is to have fun and excitement, share goals and interests for the first two years and then gradually neglect these areas." But we invite neglect into our marriage when we do not *plan* ways to have fun and excitement, share interests and set common goals.

Let me show how this works by using my exercise program as an example. I usually stay in very good shape—at least for a 40-plus-year-old. But one day I tore a muscle in my back and could not run my three miles a day or play basketball or racket ball. A few weeks later I noticed something interesting: I was beginning to breathe a little heavily just walking the two blocks from my home to the church. Then when I started to run again, I really paid the price for my six weeks of inactivity.

Those three miles seemed like 13 and my legs were very sore. Now notice what happened. I did not have to do anything to get out of shape. It took no effort on my part whatsoever. When I stopped exercising it happened naturally. The same thing occurs in marriage. We don't have to do anything to get our marriage out of shape. You can take a good marriage, neglect to exercise it by not setting mutual goals or planning for fun and excitement, and the marriage will get out of shape. And you know that once we get out of shape we invite problems into our lives.

A good friend of mine shared with me how he found this to be true in his marriage. "We thought we had the perfect marriage," he said. "It was fun and exciting at first. Then we gradually grew apart over the next 10 or 12 years. My work took a lot of time. The kids came along and my wife spent a lot of time with them. We found ourselves, after 15 years of marriage, with very little in common and facing the fact that our marriage was in trouble."

Fortunately, this couple did something about their situation. I introduced them to the idea of making their marriage relationship a priority and setting specific goals. In 15 years of marriage they had never thought of sitting down together and setting goals for their marriage. Now two years later they have an excellent relationship and goal-setting is a permanent part of their marriage.

I believe goal-setting and making specific plans to meet those goals is an answer to having fun, excitement, and sharing interests in marriage. Janet and I occasionally use part of our together time to set goals, make plans, or evaluate the progress we are making toward reaching our goals. Some goals we have reached, some we have not. Last year we set a goal of learning a sport we could do together. Another goal was to take some kind of class together. We have met the goal of learning to play a sport together (racket ball) but we still have not taken a class together.

We have a goal of doing something each year to enrich our marriage. This year we reached that goal by attending Marriage Encounter. Janet and I are preparing for the time when we will be alone. In 10 years the children will be gone and we will look at possibly 25 more years together (half of our married lives). We want to be ready. When the "empty nest" occurs many couples look at each other and see strangers. They have not developed their relationship, so when the kids are gone there are no mutual interests, no common goals, and certainly no fun and excitement. But we can plan for this not to happen. The key is to set goals now that will enable the marriage to continue to be fun after the children are gone.

Most people I know have never thought of setting specific goals for their marriage. But it really makes sense. We set goals in many other areas that are important to us: personal finances, occupations, etc. Why not set goals in the most important task we face in life—having a growing marriage?

Let me suggest one way to proceed to set goals for your marriage. I hope that having a regular together time is one goal you have already set for your marriage. That's a great start! Why not use part of that time for the next few weeks to set some additional goals?

To start, each of you make a separate list of possible goals for your marriage. Spend 30 minutes or so doing this. Next number your goals in the order of priority—#1 by the goal you think is most important and so on.

Now compare your lists and select one or two goals that you can realistically reach in the near future. Remember, a goal must be measurable, so be as specific as possible with the goals you set. If a goal is to have dinner together once a month, then get some dates down on your calendar.

Just to help you get started thinking, I will list some possible goals. Read through these and then do some creative thinking about your marriage. What things used to make your marriage fun and exciting? What do you really want for your marriage? Don't be afraid to dream a little. Write down both long- and short-range goals.

- Plan a tradition—something we can do each year.
- Select another couple to develop a close friendship with.
- Have dinner together, just the two of us, once a month. week
- Schedule a yearly planning retreat for just the two of us. Word of Life, bike trip, put swim pool / pocono NJ.
- Plan a trip to Hawaii (long-range perhaps?).
- Take a class together (cooking, photography, landscaping, etc.). computer
- Take up a sport together (jogging, tennis, racket ball, swimming, golf, etc.).
- Find one activity that can help us grow together when the children are gone.
- Walk and talk—a regular time to walk together, talking of things of interest.
- A hobby—rock hounding, mountain climbing, photography, needlepoint, etc.
- Have lunch out together once a week.
- Read a book together (perhaps one or two a year on marriage, and discuss).
- Once a year attend some type of marriage enrichment class, seminar or retreat.
- Select a ministry we can do *together* for our church (perhaps lead a small group together on the concepts presented in this manual).
- Grow together spiritually by selecting a book on

Christian living to study together—or attend a class with follow-up discussions just between the two of us.

● Share the Bible and pray together once a week.

● Start a savings account toward something we really want to do, even if it is only a dream. (Dreams sometimes come true.)

● Set financial goals for retirement.

A couple of important points to remember: (1) to share goals and interests I must be more concerned about the other person than myself; (2) select only a goal or two to start with. Don't become overly ambitious. Goal-setting is a continual process because we are continually growing and changing. There is plenty of time to set goals from now on. Select one goal, reach it successfully and then select another. One success leads to another success. By overextending we sometimes set ourselves up for failure and then want to forget the whole thing.

Goal-setting can enable you to keep your marriage full of fun, excitement, and shared interests. Keep it up!

Questions to Answer and Discuss

1. Were you surprised at how high "The loss of shared goals or interests" and "The excitement and fun has gone out of marriage," ranked on *Redbook's* list of the 10 most common marital problems? Why?

2. What three reasons does the author give to explain why the fun, excitement, shared goals and interests have gone out of many marriages? Which do you feel is most important?

3. What are some ways that neglect can creep into a marriage and cause a loss of fun, excitement, shared goals and interests?

4. What are some ways that couples can keep fun and excitement in marriage and have shared interests and goals?

5. Think back in your own marriage. What are some of the most fun and exciting times that you have had?

6. What goal have you and your spouse shared that has brought increased happiness to your marriage?

7. What do you feel prevents most couples from setting goals in their marriage?

8. Project into the future. What do you want your marriage to be like when the children are gone? Be specific.

9. Make a list of possible goals for your marriage. Number your goals in the order of priority.

10. Compare your list with your spouse's and select one goal you can realistically reach in the near future. Make specific plans to reach that goal.

If you are studying this book in a small-group session: Summarize insights you have gained into better understanding your spouse.

Notes
1. H. Norman Wright, *Communication, Key to Your Marriage* Ventura: Regal Books, 1974), p. 9.
2. Paul Tournier, *To Understand Each Other* (Atlanta: John Knox Press, 1962), p. 19.
3. *Ibid.*
4. Dennis Guernsey, *Thoroughly Married* (Dallas: Word Publishers, 1977), p. 52.
5. Bruce Narramore, *You're Someone Special* (Grand Rapids: Zondervan Publishing House, 1978), p. 16.

Section II

52
Husband-Wife
Together
Times

Together Time #1
Date: _____

"In a world in which crisis seems always imminent, the fact that love and faith keep us whole sounds a clear call to men and women ready for despair. If there is a lack of faith in ourselves and in others and, ultimately, in God, then the time has come to take stock. For faith can mean fruition in the emotional as well as the spiritual sense. Without it we are nothing."[1]

Let's Talk
1. Rate on a scale of 1-10: (1) your faith in yourself; (2) your faith in others; (3) your faith in God. Talk about it.

or

2. In what ways can a strong faith in the above three areas be shared with your children?

or

3. Your own topic.

Our thoughts:

Let's Plan (use a monthly planning calendar)
Our plans:

Let's Read God's Word (read Hebrews 11:1-16)
Important insights:

How they apply to our family:

Let's Pray
Things to pray about:

Answers we have received:

Together Time #2
Date: _____

"Family members must first have a growing relationship with Christ to have a growing relationship with one another. . . . All other relationships of life are dependent upon God's ideal—a close personal relationship with Him through Jesus Christ."[2]

Let's Talk
1. Where do you see your children in their relationship to Christ?

or

2. List one thing you could do to help family members grow closer to Christ.

or

3. Your own topic.

Our thoughts:

Let's Plan (use a monthly planning calendar)
Our plans:

Let's Read God's Word (read Ephesians 3:14-19)
Important insights:

How they apply to our family:

Let's Pray
Things to pray about:

Answers we have received:

Together Time #3
Date: _____

"Frequently people ask, 'How does one provoke children to anger?' By either over-disciplining or under-disciplining. Interestingly enough, both extremes produce the same results—insecurity."[3]

Let's Talk
1. What are some possible results of over-disciplining or under-disciplining children?

or

2. Make a statement about yourself using either the word "over-discipline" or "under-discipline." Discuss each other's statement.

or

3. Your own statement.

Our thoughts:

Let's Plan (use a monthly planning calendar)
Our plans:

Let's Read God's Word (read Ephesians 6:4)
Important insights:

How they apply to our family:

Let's Pray
Things to pray about:

Answers we have received:

Together Time #4
Date: _____

"One big bar in the mental tiger cage is called *Fear of Failure*. Nothing blocks dynamic creativity more than such a fear. Why? Because a fear of failure is really a fear of embarrassment. The need for self-esteem is one of the deepest of all human needs. To expose our self-dignity to the hazard of public ridicule is a risk we instinctively avoid! Our inclination is to play it safe and avoid the possibility of a disgrace by not even trying."[4]

Let's Talk
1. What fear of failure bothers you most? Talk about it.

or

2. What condition within your home could help family members face failure without fear?

or

3. Your own topic.

Our thoughts:

Let's Plan (use a monthly planning calendar)
Our plans:

Let's Read God's Word (read 1 John 4:18)
Important insights:

How they apply to our family:

Let's Pray
Things to pray about:

Answers we have received:

Together Time #5
Date: _____

"Adapt the training of your child so that it is in keeping with his God-given characteristics and tendencies; when he comes to maturity, he will not depart from the training he has received."[5]

Let's Talk
1. List at least three of the God-given characteristics of each of your children.

or

2. Discuss how your training takes into account your children's God-given characteristics.

or

3. Your own topic.

Our thoughts:

Let's Plan (use a monthly planning calendar)
Our plans:

Let's Read God's Word (read Proverbs 22:6)
Important insights:

How they apply to our family:

Let's Pray
Things to pray about:

Answers we have received:

Together Time #6
Date: _____

"It's tough to be a man. Despite what women claim of late—that the male animal has it all his own way and loves it—any honest man will readily confess that the masculine suit does not always fit well or comfortably. Tradition has handed him a suit of armor, in fact, an unyielding, inflexible, and often constricting mantle that cannot be stripped off without great cost to himself."[6]

Let's Talk
1. What part of the "masculine suit" do you feel is uncomfortable to wear?

or

2. Wife should share several things she appreciates about her husband's role as "man of the house."

or

3. Your own topic.

Our thoughts:

Let's Plan (use a monthly planning calendar)
Our plans:

Let's Read God's Word (read Ephesians 5:33)
Important insights:

How they apply to our family:

Let's Pray
Things to pray about:

Answers we have received:

Together Time #7
Date: _____

"God honors good thinking and human responsibility. But we can easily get into trouble because of the ego satisfaction we enjoy when we work out problems all by ourselves. On the other hand, because we often tend to be insecure and afraid of making incorrect decisions, we may withdraw and fail to fulfill our human responsibilities. It is difficult, but necessary, to maintain a balance between these two extremes.[7]

Let's Talk
1. Each share, of the two extremes mentioned above, which way do you tend to lean?

or

2. How would you like to make family decisions?

or

3. Your own topic.

Our thoughts:

Let's Plan (use a monthly planning calendar)
Our plans:

Let's Read God's Word (read James 4:13-17; Proverbs 16:1-3)
Important insights:

How they apply to our family:

Let's Pray
Things to pray about:

Answers we have received:

Together Time #8
Date: _____

"Through these brief forays into the responsibilities of motherhood and from the experience gained in counseling women, I have developed a deep appreciation for the unique skills required of wives and mothers. In my view their job is of utmost importance to the health and vitality of our society and I regret the lack of respect and status given today's 'housewives.' "[8]

Let's Talk
1. What do you hear the media saying about the importance of the "housewife" today? How do you feel about what is said?

or

2. Husband should share with his wife several things he appreciates about her work at home.

or

3. Your own topic.

Our thoughts:

Let's Plan (use a monthly planning calendar)
Our plans:

Let's Read God's Word (read Proverbs 31:10)
Important insights:

How they apply to our family:

Let's Pray
Things to pray about:

Answers we have received:

Together Time #9
Date: _____

"Explosive anger is powerless to effect change in relationships. . . . Vented anger may ventilate feelings and provide instant though temporary release for tortured emotions, but it does little for relationships. Clearly suppressed anger is something different. Clear statement of anger feelings and angry demands can slice through emotional barriers or communications tangles and establish contact."[9]

Let's Talk
1. Think of examples in your family of the two ways of handling anger mentioned above.

or

2. In what ways are you satisfied or dissatisfied in the way that anger is handled in your home?

or

3. Your own topic.

Our thoughts:

Let's Plan (use a monthly planning calendar)
Our plans:

Let's Read God's Word (read Mark 3:1-6; Ephesians
4:26; Proverbs 15:18; Galatians 5:19-21)
Important insights:

How they apply to our family:

Let's Pray
Things to pray about:

Answers we have received:

Together Time #10
Date: _____

"Why are our values so crucial to the moral development of our children? Because of a process called 'identification.' Both consciously and unconsciously, children want to be like their mothers and fathers. This process is known as identification or internalization. In it children gradually take on their parents' attitudes and values; they become increasingly like their parents."[10]

Let's Talk
1. Share an attitude or value that you have seen in your children that is like your own.

or

2. What implications does the statement above have for your attitudes and values?

or

3. Your own topic.
Our thoughts:

Let's Plan (use a monthly planning calendar)
Our plans:

Let's Read God's Word (read Ephesians 5:1; Luke 6:40)
Important insights:

How they apply to our family:

Let's Pray
Things to pray about:

Answers we have received:

Together Time #11
Date: _____

You have heard that "the family that prays together stays together." It is important for the family that prays together to pray for one another. Love and understanding flourish when each person prays for the other daily.

Let's Talk
1. Why do you feel a family could be drawn closer together through praying for one another?

or

2. Think of some ways to encourage family members to pray for one another. Pray for each family member together.

or

3. Your own topic.

Our thoughts:

Let's Plan (use a monthly planning calendar)
Our plans:

Let's Read God's Word (read Philippians 1:3-11)
Important insights:

How they apply to our family:

Let's Pray
Things to pray about:

Answers we have received:

Together Time #12
Date: _____

Last night I asked our family to pray for a 15-year-old girl in the church whose parents had just disowned her. They took her belongings to the Good Will and sold her 10-speed bike. The parents want no trace of her in their lives. Heidi, our 13-year-old daughter said, "But, Dad, that's conditional love." "Yes it is," I replied, "but God's love is forever and so is ours for you."

Let's Talk
1. Why is it essential that children understand unconditional love?

or

2. What are some ways you can reinforce the concept of unconditional love in the lives of your children?

or

3. Your own topic.

Our thoughts:

Let's Plan (use a monthly planning calendar)
Our plans:

Let's Read God's Word (read 1 John 4:7-21)
Important insights:

How they apply to our family:

Let's Pray
Things to pray about:

Answers we have received:

Together Time #13
Date: _____

"The time to be happy is *now*. The place to be happy is *here*. The way to be happy is to *make others happy*."[11]

Let's Talk
1. On a scale of 1-10 rate the "happiness" atmosphere of your home.

or

2. Discuss some ways to make your home a happier place.

or

3. Your own topic.

Our thoughts:

Let's Plan (use a monthly planning calendar)
Our plans:

Let's Read God's Word (read Proverbs 15:30; Psalms 118:24)
Important insights:

How they apply to our family:

Let's Pray
Things to pray about:

Answers we have received:

Together Time #14
Date: _____

In our home each week on Family Night, we honor a different family member. Love and appreciation are expressed in a variety of ways to make the "honoree" feel special. I feel that honoring one another in special ways should be an integral part of every home.

Let's Talk
1. What kinds of things could be done to help you feel honored?

or

2. Think of some ideas of how members of your family could be honored.

or

3. Your own topic.

Our thoughts:

Let's Plan (use a monthly planning calendar)
Our plans:

Let's Read God's Word (read Romans 12:10)
Important insights:

How they apply to our family:

Let's Pray
Things to pray about:

Answers we have received:

Together Time #15
Date: _____

"But it is true, I believe, that too many men do not understand the emotional needs of their wives. They live in a vastly different world of their own with ample frustrations of their own. Either they are unable to put themselves in a woman's place, seeing and feeling what she experiences, or else they are preoccupied with their own work and simply aren't listening."[12]

Let's Talk
1. How do you feel about the above statement and why?

or

2. Share two emotional needs that you would like more fully understood.

or

3. Your own topic.

Our thoughts:

Let's Plan (use a monthly planning calendar)
Our plans:

Let's Read God's Word (read 1 Peter 3:7)
Important insights:

How they apply to our family:

Let's Pray
Things to pray about:

Answers we have received:

Together Time #16
Date: _____

Real love is much more than a feeling or an emotion. It is something you do.

Let's Talk
1. Discuss a couple you know who demonstrate real love in their marriage.

or

2. Discuss the statement about love at the top of this page.

or

3. Your own topic.

Our thoughts:

Let's Plan (use a monthly planning calendar)
Our plans:

Let's Read God's Word (read 1 Corinthians 13)
Important insights:

How they apply to our family:

Let's Pray
Things to pray about:

Answers we have received:

Together Time #17
Date: _____

It is within the family that training for real friendship should happen. The curriculum is loyalty, acceptance, bringing out the best and confronting in love—lived out at home.

Let's Talk
1. In the quality of friendship mentioned above which do you feel is most important? Which is your strength?

or

2. What could be done in your home to encourage family members to become better friends?

or

3. Your own topic.

Our thoughts:

Let's Plan (use a monthly planning calendar)
Our plans:

Let's Read God's Word (read Proverbs 17:7; 18:24)
Important insights:

How they apply to our family:

Let's Pray
Things to pray about:

Answers we have received:

Together Time #18
Date: _____

"To achieve understanding we need to accept our natural differences."[13]

Let's Talk
1. Do you agree or disagree with the above statement? Why?

or

2. Each name two natural differences in the other. Have you accepted these? Has it increased understanding?

or

3. Your own topic.

Our thoughts:

Let's Plan (use a monthly planning calendar)
Our plans:

Let's Read God's Word (read Ephesians 4:1,2)
Important insights:

How they apply to our family:

Let's Pray
Things to pray about:

Answers we have received:

Together Time #19
Date: _____

"Remember that actions speak louder than words; non-verbal communication is more important than verbal communication."[14]

Let's Talk
1. Each share a personal action that drowns out your words.

or

2. Do you agree or disagree with the above statement? Use an illustration to explain why.

or

3. Your own topic.

Our thoughts:

Let's Plan (use a monthly planning calendar)
Our plans:

Let's Read God's Word (read 1 John 3:18)
Important insights:

How they apply to our family:

Let's Pray
Things to pray about:

Answers we have received:

Together Time #20
Date: _____

"It is obvious that God, the master builder of homes . . . wants His carpenters, Christian parents, to put in a full shift using the correct tools, including His Word."[15]

Let's Talk
1. What important tools has God put at the disposal of us as Christian parents?

or

2. What evidence is there in our children that God is using us to build Christian character in them?

or

3. Your own topic.

Our thoughts:

Let's Plan (use a monthly planning calendar)
Our plans:

Let's Read God's Word (read Psalm 127)
Important insights:

How they apply to our family:

Let's Pray
Things to pray about:

Answers we have received:

Together Time #21
Date: _____

"Lovemaking in its proper context involves the entire process of communication. This is where lovemaking in a Christian marriage differs from lovemaking in another context. To the Christian, lovemaking is not only a physical act, it is an event. To become a successful lover is to become a person who is able to relate to your partner in the totality of your personality."[16]

Let's Talk
1. Discuss the above statement. Is relating to your partner in the "totality of your personality" really that important to sexual fulfillment? Why?

or

2. What area of sex is most difficult for you to talk about?

or

3. Your own topic.

Our thoughts:

Let's Plan (use a monthly planning calendar)
Our plans:

Let's Read God's Word (read 1 Corinthians 7:1-5)
Important insights:

How they apply to our family:

Let's Pray
Things to pray about:

Answers we have received:

Together Time #22
Date:_____

In our society the young and the old rarely meet for meaningful interaction. Older persons are treated as outdated relics with little to offer in a sophisticated space age. And yet it is that sharing between the ages that gives the younger wisdom, confidence in the future and a bridge to the past—and the older a sense of worth.

Let's Talk
1. What older persons have influenced you significantly?

or

2. Think of some ways your family could increase its interaction with older persons.

or

3. Your own topic.

Our thoughts:

Let's Plan (use a monthly planning calendar)
Our plans:

Let's Read God's Word (read Psalms 92:12; 103:5;
Exodus 20:12)
Important insights:

How they apply to our family:

Let's Pray
Things to pray about:

Answers we have received:

Together Time #23
Date:_____

"Forgiveness costs; especially in marriage when it means accepting instead of demanding repayment for a wrong done; where it means releasing the other instead of exacting revenge; where it means reaching out in love instead of relishing resentments. It costs to forgive." [17]

Let's Talk

1. Complete the statement: The most difficult part of forgiveness for me is: _____ .

or

2. Who is the most forgiving person you have ever known?

or

3. Your own topic.

Our thoughts:

Let's Plan (use a monthly planning calendar)
Our plans:

Let's Read God's Word (Read Ephesians 4:31,32)
Important insights:

How they apply to our family:

Let's Pray
Things to pray about:

Answers we have received:

Together Time #24
Date:_____

"Nothing cools friendship so quickly as failure to be in touch with joys and sorrows, or being judgmental."[18]

Let's Talk
1. Share a feeling that you would like your spouse to be in touch with.

or

2. Why is it that we many times fail to be in touch with the feelings of others?

or

3. Your own topic.

Our thoughts:

Let's Plan (use a monthly planning calendar)
Our plans:

Let's Read God's Word (read Romans 12:15)
Important insights:

How they apply to our family:

Let's Pray
Things to pray about:

Answers we have received:

Together Time #25
Date:_____

"What happens when the family eats together—
especially at the dinner hour—is an extremely important
part of building family unity and teaching Christian values. By conversation at the dinner hour, listening, sharing, communicating ideas and dreams, the family circle is
drawn together with love and understanding."[19]

Let's Talk

1. Is our family circle drawn tighter together with love
and understanding at the dinner hour?

or

2. What steps could we take to use our table time to
bring the family closer together?

or

3. Your own topic.

Our thoughts:

Let's Plan (use a monthly planning calendar)
Our plans:

Let's Read God's Word (read Proverbs 15:17; 17:1)
Important insights:

How they apply to our family:

Let's Pray
Things to pray about:

Answers we have received:

Together Time #26
Date:_____

"To provide for your family involves more than the provision of food and shelter. It involves your active, concerned participation in their lives, especially [in] your wife's [life]. If a husband doesn't he's judged by God to be worse than an infidel."[20]

Let's Talk
1. Both share how you feel about the amount of time you spend together.

or

2. Ask your wife how you can participate more fully in her and the children's lives.

or

3. Your own topic.

Our thoughts:

Let's Plan (use a monthly planning calendar)
Our plans:

Let's Read God's Word (read 1 Timothy 5:8)
Important insights:

How they apply to our family:

Let's Pray
Things to pray about:

Answers we have received:

Together Time #27
Date:_____

Words have great power. They have provoked war, broken marriages and caused great personal pain. Words have stopped wars, mended marriages and healed great hurts. It is awesome to think that God has entrusted to us such a powerful force, both good and evil. How words are used within the family will influence not only family success but our children's relationship with others as well.

Let's Talk
1. Each give an example of how you have seen words bring either hurt or healing to a relationship.

or

2. Each share some words you often use that would be better not said.

or

3. Your own topic.

Our thoughts:

Let's Plan (use a monthly planning calendar)
Our plans:

Let's Read God's Word (read Proverbs 12:18; 29:20;
11:9; 18:8; 13:3; 21:23; 15:1; 15:4)
Important insights:

How they apply to our family:

Let's Pray
Things to pray about:

Answers we have received:

Together Time #28
Date:_____

"Love and unity, like other characteristics of the healthy Christian family, are the result of specific things parents decide to work at and do."[21]

Let's Talk
1. What indication do we have in our home that love and unity are strong?

or

2. What things weaken love and unity in our home?

or

3. Your own topic.

Our thoughts:

Let's Plan (use a monthly planning calendar)
Our plans:

Let's Read God's Word (read Proverbs 24:3,4)
Important insights:

How they apply to our family:

Let's Pray
Things to pray about:

Answers we have received:

Together Time #29
Date:————————

"As Christian parents we need to plan for ways our homes can become 'nurture centers' for our children. God wants parents to pass on to each of their children their own faith and experience of God's love and care."[22]

Let's Talk
1. In what specific ways are you passing on your faith and experience of God's love to your children?

                    or

2. Each think of one way you can make your home a more effective "nurture center" for your children.

                    or

3. Your own topic.

Our thoughts:

Let's Plan (use a monthly planning calendar)
Our plans:

Let's Read God's Word (read Deuteronomy 6:4-9)
Important insights:

How they apply to our family:

Let's Pray
Things to pray about:

Answers we have received:

Together Time #30
Date:_____

"The foundation for moral and spiritual training is our own set of priorities. There come times for each of us when we need to reflect carefully our own style of living and ask ourselves some fundamental questions. For us as Christian parents, one of these questions should surely be 'What are the most important things in life to me?' "[23]

Let's Talk
1. List the priorities that are helping you in the moral and spiritual training of your children.

or

2. List the priorities that are hindering you in the moral and spiritual training of your children.

or

3. Your own topic.

Our thoughts:

Let's Plan (use a monthly planning calendar)
Our plans:

Let's Read God's Word (read Matthew 6:24-34)
Important insights:

How they apply to our family:

Let's Pray
Things to pray about:

Answers we have received:

Together Time #31
Date:_____

"In today's world, parents find themselves at the mercy of a society which imposes pressures and priorities that allow neither time nor place for meaningful activities and relations between children and adults, which downgrade the role of parents and the functions of parenthood, and which prevent the parent from doing things he wants to do as a guide, friend, and companion to his children."[24]

Let's Talk
1. What pressures do you feel society is putting on your family?

or

2. What can you do about the pressures society puts on your family?

or

3. Your own topic.

Our thoughts:

Let's Plan (use a monthly planning calendar)
Our plans:

Let's Read God's Word (read Romans 12:1,2)
Important insights:

How they apply to our family:

Let's Pray
Things to pray about:

Answers we have received:

Together Time #32
Date:_____

"Of all human relationships, marriage succeeds in developing maturity that can't be obtained in any other social relationship."[25]

Let's Talk
1. Each share one area of your life that is more mature because of your marriage.

or

2. What area of your life would you like to see become more mature?

or

3. Your own topic.

Our thoughts:

Let's Plan (use a monthly planning calendar)
Our plans:

Let's Read God's Word (read Genesis 2:18-25)
Important insights:

How they apply to our family:

Let's Pray
Things to pray about:

Answers we have received:

Together Time #33
Date:_____

"It has been said that a fulfilled marriage can come only when each partner grows because of the union, . . . the potential for growth that lies within both husband and wife needs encouragement for the marriage to blossom."[26]

Let's Talk
1. Share a way in which your spouse has encouraged you to reach your true potential.

or

2. Share an area of potential growth in your spouse.

or

3. Your own topic.

Our thoughts:

Let's Plan (use a monthly planning calendar)
Our plans:

Let's Read God's Word (read 1 Thessalonians 5:11)
Important insights:

How they apply to our family:

Let's Pray
Things to pray about:

Answers we have received:

Together Time #34
Date:_____

"Understanding in a marriage doesn't mean that there are no differences. It does mean that you and your mate are able to talk about the differences and come to an understanding of each other's views."[27]

Let's Talk
1. Each share an area where you would like to be understood more fully.

or

2. An area in which I feel fully understood is _____ .

or

3. Your own topic.

Our thoughts:

Let's Plan (use a monthly planning calendar)
Our plans:

Let's Read God's Word (read Philippians 2:1-11)
Important insights:

How they apply to our family:

Let's Pray
Things to pray about:

Answers we have received:

Together Time #35
Date:_____

"As head, a husband serves his family by giving them intelligent, sensitive leadership. His headship is not meant for domineering and stifling his wife and children, but for leading, protecting, providing and caring for them."[28]

Let's Talk
1. Each write a paragraph on what you feel it means to be the "*head*" of the home.

or

2. On the above statement about leadership, what do you strongly agree or disagree with?

or

3. Your own topic.

Our thoughts:

Let's Plan (use a monthly planning calendar)
Our plans:

Let's Read God's Word (read Ephesians 5:21-33)
Important insights:

How they apply to our family:

Let's Pray
Things to pray about:

Answers we have received:

Together Time #36
Date: _____

"Submission is not the exclusive responsibility of the woman. Submission is the life-style of the Christian. To the woman the question is, 'Are you willing to submit yourself, not first of all to your husband, but to the Lord's plan for your functioning in marital relationship?' "[29]

Let's Talk
1. Each define submission. In what ways is it important in your marriage relationship?

or

2. Share your feelings about submission.

or

3. Your own topic.

Our thoughts:

Let's Plan (use a monthly planning calendar)
Our plans:

Let's Read God's Word (read Ephesians 5:21-33)
Important insights:

How they apply to our family:

Let's Pray
Things to pray about:

Answers we have received:

Together Time #37
Date: _____

"The fact that *discipline* and *disciple* come from the same root word is suggestive of the positive meaning of discipline. Anyone can punish a child but only those who can make disciples of the children can truly discipline them."[30]

Let's Talk
1. What changes would have to be made in your home if you followed the above principles?

or

2. Each rate yourself in your ability to use positive discipline. How can a parent "disciple" his children?

or

3. Your own topic.

Our thoughts:

Let's Plan (use a monthly planning calendar)
Our plans:

Let's Read God's Word (read Hebrews 12:7-11)
Important insights:

How they apply to our family:

Let's Pray
Things to pray about:

Answers we have received:

Together Time #38
Date: _____

"I can come to see conflict as natural, neutral, normal. I may be able to see the difficulties we experience as tensions in relationships and honest differences in perspective that can be worked through by caring about each other and each comforting the other with truth expressed by love."[31]

Let's Talk
1. Each list one thing you find difficult to confront the other with.

or

2. Discuss the above statements. Do you agree or disagree?

or

3. Your own topic.

Our thoughts:

Let's Plan (use a monthly planning calendar)
Our plans:

Let's Read God's Word (read Ephesians 4:15,16)
Important insights:

How they apply to our family:

Let's Pray
Things to pray about:

Answers we have received:

Together Time #39
Date: _____

"Paul says, 'Don't worry, ask God for what you need . . . and then . . . always asking him with a thankful heart.' We ask for what He has guided us to ask in keeping with His will. After that we give thanks that He has heard us and the matter is being worked out according to His timing, planning, and purpose. I used to ask, worry, and ask again as if God were hard of hearing. Now I am trying to learn how to ask once and thank Him repeatedly."[32]

Let's Talk
1. What worry have you been harboring that you can give to God?

or

2. What truth from the above statement can you apply to your situation?

or

3. Your own topic.

Our thoughts:

Let's Plan (use a monthly planning calendar)
Our plans:

Let's Read God's Word (read Philippians 4:6)
Important insights:

How they apply to our family:

Let's Pray
Things to pray about:

Answers we have received:

Together Time #40
Date: _____

"Lord, toughen my faith. I am soft and sentimental and want a magic escape from difficulties. I surrender all the sticky problems, the frustrating people, the impossible situations to you and ask you to help me grow through them. Then, help me to be sensitive to share what you have given to me with the people who struggle and long for meaning all around me. Amen."[33]

Let's Talk

1. Finish the sentence, My biggest problem with difficult situations is _____ .

or

2. Talk about some difficult situations you have experienced that could help you minister to others.

or

3. Your own topic.

Our thoughts:

Let's Plan (use a monthly planning calendar)
Our plans:

Let's Read God's Word (read James 1:1-8)
Important insights:

How they apply to our family:

Let's Pray
Things to pray about:

Answers we have received:

Together Time #41
Date: _____

"Children often con us into doing their work or failing to carry out needed discipline by playing on our consciences. By making us feel, 'I guess I'm being a little firm,' or 'I sure hate to see him suffer that way,' they get us where they want us! Not being able to tolerate the guilty feeling, we give in."[34]

Let's Talk
1. In what circumstances do you usually feel guilty when dealing with your children?

or

2. Exchange ideas on ways to overcome guilt.

or

3. Your own topic.

Our thoughts:

Let's Plan (use a monthly planning calendar)
Our plans:

Let's Read God's Word (read Romans 8:1)
Important insights:

How they apply to our family:

Let's Pray
Things to pray about:

Answers we have received:

Together Time #42
Date: _____

It is an interesting fact that many times we fail to communicate love and appreciation to those who are closest to us—our spouse and children.

Let's Talk
1. Each rate yourself on a scale of 1-10 on how well you feel you communicate love and appreciation to others in the family.

or

2. Take time now to say three things you appreciate about each other.

or

3. Your own topic.

Our thoughts:

Let's Plan (use a monthly planning calendar)
Our plans:

Let's Read God's Word (read Colossians 3:12-14)
Important insights:

How they apply to our family:

Let's Pray
Things to pray about:

Answers we have received:

Together Time #43
Date: _____

Marriage is not as much a matter of finding the right person but deciding to become the right person. What kind of a person are you willing to become?

Let's Talk
1. Discuss strengths you bring into our marriage/ weaknesses I bring into our marriage.

or

2. Discuss why you believe the above statement to be true or false.

or

3. Your own topic.

Our thoughts:

Let's Plan (use a monthly planning calendar)
Our plans:

Let's Read God's Word (read 2 Peter 1:1-11)
Important insights:

How they apply to our family:

Let's Pray
Things to pray about:

Answers we have received:

Together Time #44
Date: _____

"I believe that *families serving others* needs to be an integral philosophy of the church. We are reborn to serve."[35]

Let's Talk

1. Is serving others a high priority in our family?

or

2. What is one way our family could serve others now?

or

3. Your own topic.

Our thoughts:

Let's Plan (use a monthly planning calendar)
Our plans:

Let's Read God's Word (read Matthew 25:31-46)
Important insights:

How they apply to our family:

Let's Pray
Things to pray about:

Answers we have received:

Together Time #45
Date: _____

"Entertaining says, 'I want to impress you with my beautiful home, my clever decorating, my gourmet cooking.'
Hospitality, however, seeks to minister. It says, 'This
home is not mine. It is truly a gift from my master. I am
his servant and I use it as he desires.' "[36]

Let's Talk
1. Do you use your home for "entertaining" or for "hospitality"?

or

2. What can we do to be more hospitable?

or

3. Your own topic.

Our thoughts:

Let's Plan (use a monthly planning calendar)
Our plans:

Let's Read God's Word (read 1 Peter 4:9)
Important insights:

How they apply to our family:

Let's Pray
Things to pray about:

Answers we have received:

Together Time #46
Date: _____

"When instituting marriage, God declared, 'They shall no longer be two, but one.' To be one obviously means not to have secrets from each other. As soon as couples begin to hide matters from one another they compromise the basic oneness of marriage."[37]

Let's Talk

1. Do you have a secret you could share now with your spouse?

or

2. What prevents us from being completely open in marriage?

or

3. Your own topic.

Our thoughts:

Let's Plan (use a monthly planning calendar)
Our plans:

Let's Read God's Word (read Mark 10:6-9)
Important insights:

How they apply to our family:

Let's Pray
Things to pray about:

Answers we have received:

Together Time #47
Date: _____

"Someone has suggested that listening intently with one's mouth shut is a basic communication skill needed in marriages. Think about your own communication pattern. Do you listen? How much of what is said do you hear? It has been estimated that usually a person hears only about 20 percent of what is said."[38]

Let's Talk
1. Each rate yourself as a listener on a scale of 1 to 10.

or

2. Each complete the sentence: As a listener I _____ .

or

3. Your own topic.

Our thoughts:

Let's Plan (use a monthly planning calendar)
Our plans:

Let's Read God's Word (read James 1:19)
Important insights:

How they apply to our family:

Let's Pray
Things to pray about:

Answers we have received:

Together Time #48
Date: _____

"Since the family in the New Testament is in reality the church in miniature, it follows naturally that the maturity level of a Christian family can also be determined by the degree of faith, hope, and love expressed by that family as a whole—particularly on the part of Dad, Mom, and older children."[39]

Let's Talk
1. How does your family rank in the areas of faith, hope, and love?

or

2. How do you as parents rank in each of those areas? What can you do to help your family grow in faith, hope and love?

or

3. Your own topic.

Our thoughts:

Let's Plan (use a monthly planning calendar)
Our plans:

Let's Read God's Word (read 1 Thessalonians 1:2,3)
Important insights:

How they apply to our family:

Let's Pray
Things to pray about:

Answers we have received:

Together Time #49
Date: _____

One of the greatest gifts we can give our children is an excitement about God's Word and how it can guide their lives. But to do this our children must first see that we value God's Word. Our own personal devotions, family Bible reading, Bible memorization, and encouraging our children to have quiet times are ways to reach this goal.

Let's Talk
1. Do your children value God's Word? Why or why not?

or

2. Agree on one thing you can do this week to help your children become more excited about God's Word.

or

3. Your own topic.

Our thoughts:

Let's Plan (use a monthly planning calendar)
Our plans:

Let's Read God's Word (read 2 Timothy 3:16,17)
Important insights:

How they apply to our family:

Let's Pray
Things to pray about:

Answers we have received:

Together Time #50
Date: _____

One of the biggest obstacles to having a Christ-centered family is the many things that compete for our time and interest. I believe one of Satan's greatest tools is diversion. He can keep us so busy and fragmented that we lose our focus on Christ and our family.

Let's Talk
1. What are some things that compete for your family's time and interest?

or

2. What changes in your family life need to be made so you can sharpen your focus on Christ?

or

3. Your own topic.

Our thoughts:

Let's Plan (use a monthly planning calendar)
Our plans:

Let's Read God's Word (read Colossians 3:1-4)
Important insights:

How they apply to our family:

Let's Pray
Things to pray about:

Answers we have received:

Together Time #51
Date: _____

One of the greatest gifts we can give our children is a healthy sense of self-esteem. When our children feel that they are very special to God and to us, they are better able to withstand the negative forces of society which can undermine their self-esteem.

Let's Talk
1. On a scale of 1-10 rate how each of your children feels about himself/herself.

or

2. One way we can help our children have a better self-image is _____ .

or

3. Your own topic.

Our thoughts:

Let's Plan (use a monthly planning calendar)
Our plans:

Let's Read God's Word (read Psalm 139)
Important insights:

How they apply to our family:

Let's Pray
Things to pray about:

Answers we have received:

Together Time #52
Date: _____

Criticism within the family can be very destructive. Many times we use criticism to build ourselves up while over-looking what it does to the other person. Within a marriage criticism is especially damaging. God wants our marriages to be sources of encouragement.

Let's Talk
1. When do you feel most critical?

or

2. What is a valid alternative to criticism within a marriage?

or

3. Your own topic.

Our thoughts:

Let's Plan (use a monthly planning calendar)
Our plans:

Let's Read God's Word (read Galatians 5:13-15 from
The Living Bible)
Important insights:

How they apply to our family:

Let's Pray
Things to pray about:

Answers we have received:

Notes

1. Norman Vincent Peale and Smiley Blanton, *Faith Is the Answer* (Carmel, NY: Guideposts Associates, Inc., 1955), p. 3.

2. Wayne Rickerson, *How to Help the Christian Home* (Ventura, CA: Regal Books, 1976), p. 15.

3. Howard G. Hendricks, *Heaven Help the Home* (Wheaton, IL: Scripture Press, 1973), p. 67.

4. Robert H. Schuller, *You Can Become the Person You Want to Be* (New York: W. Clement Stone, Publisher, 1973), p. 5.

5. Charles R. Swindoll, *You and Your Child* (Nashville: Thomas Nelson, Inc., 1977), p. 27.

6. James L. Johnson, *What Every Woman Should Know About a Man* (Grand Rapids: Zondervan Publishing House, 1977), p. 11.

7. Gene A. Getz, *Abraham, Trials and Triumphs* (Ventura, CA: Regal Books, 1976), p. 34.

8. James Dobson, *What Wives Wish Their Husbands Knew About Women* (Wheaton, IL: Tyndale House Publishers, Inc., 1975), pp. 11,12.

9. David Augsburger, *Caring Enough to Confront* (Ventura, CA: Regal Books, 1974), p. 41.

10. Wayne Rickerson, *Getting Your Family Together* (Ventura, CA: Regal Books, 1976), p. 38.

11. Author unknown.

12. Dobson, *What Wives Wish . . .* , p. 13.

13. Paul Tournier, *To Understand Each Other* (Atlanta: John Knox Press, 1976), p. 36.

14. Sven Wahlroos, *Family Communication* (New York: New American Library, Inc., 1976), p. 8.

15. Rickerson, *Getting Your Family Together*, p. 9.

16. Dennis Guernsey, *Thoroughly Married* (Waco, TX: Word, Inc., 1975), pp. 31,32.

17. David W. Augsburger, *Cherishable: Love and Marriage* (Scottdale, PA: Herald Press Books, 1971), pp. 141,142.

18. Joan Jacobs, *Feelings: Where They Come From and How to Handle Them* (Wheaton, IL: Tyndale House Publishers, 1976), p. 19.

19. Rickerson, *Getting Your Family Together*, p. 57.

20. Guernsey, *Thoroughly Married*, p. 57.

21. Norm Wakefield, *You Can Have a Happier Family* (Ventura, CA: Regal Books, 1977), p. 14.

22. Wayne Rickerson, *Good Times for Your Family* (Ventura, CA: Regal Books, 1975), p. 17.

23. Bruce Narramore, *An Ounce of Prevention* (Grand Rapids: Zondervan Publishing House, 1973), p. 26.

24. Urie Bronfenbrenner, *Two Worlds of Childhood* (New York: Simon and Schuster, 1972), pp. xiii, xiv.

25. Celestial Seasoning, Inc., 1975.

26. Judson J. Swihart, *How Do You Say "I Love You?"* (Downers Grove, IL: Inter-Varsity Press, 1977), pp. 66,67.

27. H. Norman Wright, *Communication: Key to Your Marriage* (Ventura, CA: Regal Books, 1974), Intro.

28. Larry and Nordis Christenson, *The Christian Couple* (Minneapolis:

Bethany Fellowship, Inc., 1977), p. 125.
29. Hendricks, *Heaven Help the Home*, p. 31.
30. Charles R. Swindoll, *You and Your Child* (Nashville: Thomas Nelson, Inc., 1977), p. 89.
31. Augsburger, *Caring Enough to Confront*, p. 4.
32. Lloyd John Ogilvie, *Let God Love You* (Waco, TX: Word, Inc., 1974), p. 142.
33. Ibid., p. 40.
34. Bruce Narramore, *A Guide to Child Rearing* (Grand Rapids: Zondervan Publishing House, 1972), p. 143.
35. Rickerson, *How to Help the Christian Home*, p. 126.
36. Karen Burton Mains, *Open Heart, Open Home* (Elgin, IL: David C. Cook Publishing Co., 1976), p. 25.
37. Tournier, *To Understand Each Other*, p. 15.
38. Wright, *Communication*, p. 55.
39. Gene A. Getz, *The Measure of a Family* (Ventura, CA: Regal Books, 1976), p. 14.

Section III

How
to
Help
Couples
in
Your
Church

PASS IT ON

You and your spouse have read this book. You have started Together Times. You are beginning to experience the growth and closeness you've always wanted in your marriage. Now is the time to help others have happy, close marriages. *PASS IT ON*. I believe that it is couples like you, who are committed to growth in your own marriage, that will enable other couples to build happy, close marriages.

Couple to Couple

Can you think of another couple that you feel would be open to starting Together Times in their marriage? Why not invite them to your house and share with them the benefits of these communication dates. Give them a gift of a copy of this book. Schedule another get-together in a month to see how they are doing. When they are going strong, find another couple and repeat the procedure.

Couple to Couples
(Small-Group Sharing)

I believe one of the best ways to help Christian couples is in the atmosphere of the small group. When four or five couples get together weekly for eight weeks to share about their marriages, significant growth can occur.

But you say, "I've never led a small group. I wouldn't be qualified." Your greatest qualification for leading a small group is that you are committed and learning to be open and accepting in your own marriage. These qualities are necessary for a couple to successfully lead a group. I have found that couples who are committed to growth in their own marriages—with a few simple guidelines—can successfully lead other couples in small groups.

How to Get Started: First, you find three or four other couples that are willing to commit themselves to eight weeks in a small group for the purpose of improving their marriage. Explain that they must be willing to commit themselves to attend all eight sessions, to read a chapter in the book, and to prepare for class by sharing answers to some questions.

How to Lead the Group: It is important to get a clear picture of how you will function as leader. First of all, you are not a marriage expert sharing your great knowledge with other, less fortunate couples. You are simply a couple, like the others present, who is working at having a growing marriage. This takes the pressure off you as a leader and also frees others to share their own strengths and weaknesses.

Except for the first session, couples will have prepared themselves for sharing by completing the question sheets at the end of each chapter. As a leader, you and your spouse need to fill out the same sheet. This will be your only preparation for the session. At the start of each session, after some informal chitchat, announce the topic and ask the first question. For the first couple of sessions it may be wise for you to be the first to share. Try not to share anything too dramatic because others might see that as a "hard act to follow."

It is best to allow others to share about the questions as they feel ready. In other words, don't go around the circle or call names. People are in various stages of sharing, from the very open to the very reserved. Respect where they are and give them space to grow in openness. There will be times of awkward silence. Resist the temptation to "jump in" and rescue the situation by monologuing.

As a general rule try not to let the sharing drift too far from the questions. There will be digression, for sure. This is healthy. For example, one question might touch off sharing in related areas. Use your own judgment on when to bring things back to the basic question or when to move on to the next question.

At times there will be joking and laughing about certain areas. This is good and necessary. It relieves the tension that can build. Look at these times as welcome guests and then move back to the serious side of the topic. If persons are not responding well to a question, feel free to move on to the next one.

Some persons (usually men) will want to argue about the way some of the questions are phrased. This, many times, is a way of not dealing with the question. With this in mind, try to move quickly from a critical analysis of the way the question is stated to the sharing.

Try to move from the head ("this is what I think") to the heart ("this is the way I feel"). Learning to share feelings is what your group is all about.

Following is an outline of your eight group sessions.

Session 1: This is an introductory session. Ask couples in advance to bring one or two of their wedding pictures and be ready to share how they met and a little about their wedding.

Start the session by having each person introduce himself and tell a little about his family. Then have each couple show their wedding pictures and tell a little about their wedding.

Next, hand out the books and explain the ground rules for your group. Have each couple check their calendars and make sure they can attend all eight sessions. A rule of thumb that we have used is that if a couple already knows they will miss a session, it would be better for them to wait for a later group.

Each couple is to do the required reading and questions *before* each session. Couples are not to compare answers before the session. Start on time and end on time. We find that an hour-and-a-half session, and then refreshments, works well. Resist the temptation to go over your time when the session is going well. It is not necessary to discuss every question at every session!

Emphasize that the purpose of the group session is to gain a better understanding of a person's spouse and of himself. Anything said within the group is strictly confidential.

Answer any questions persons might have about the group and then lead the following activities:

1. Have each person share his biggest surprise about marriage.

2. Each person may ask one question of someone else in the group.

3. Have each person give his mate's outstanding quality.

4. Have each person describe the ideal marriage.

5. Have each person write a definition of a Christian marriage. Have persons share these definitions. Decide as a group on some essential elements of such a definition. Conclude by reading the following definition of a Christian marriage by H. Norman Wright:

A Christian marriage is a total commitment of two people to the person of Jesus Christ and one another. It is a commitment in which there is no holding back of anything. A Christian marriage is similar to a solvent, a feeling of the man and woman to be themselves and become all that God intends for them to become. Marriage is the refining process that God will use to have us develop into the men and women He wants us to become. [1]

Assign chapter 1 and the corresponding questions.

Prayer should be a part of all sessions. Some groups might want to open or close with prayer. Other groups might want to use conversational prayer as a part of the session. In a group of which I was a part each couple wrote their names on a slip of paper. We then drew names and prayed for that couple during the next week. We repeated this process each time we met. Be sure your group feels comfortable with the way you handle prayer in your session.

Sessions 2-7: Sessions 2-7 are similar. Each of these sessions covers one of the six steps in the book. To prepare for a session, each person reads the appropriate section and answers the questions at the end.

After some chitchat at the beginning of your session, simply ask the first questions. As I mentioned before, the first couple of sessions you might want to share first to break the ice. Your openness will encourage others to be open. Continue to use the questions as a means to facilitate sharing.

Only the first eight questions following each step are for use in your group. Questions 9 and 10 are for couples to complete at home and then share with each other. This is their commitment to change. Remember that the purpose of these sessions is to increase understanding. Real understanding within marriage means change.

It is not necessary for couples to share with the group their answers to 9 and 10. Explain, however, that couples are to share the content of these questions and their summary of insights with each other during the week.

In addition to the questions for Steps 3-6 have couples share how their together times are going.

Session 8: Explain to your group that session 8 is going to be an informal time to discuss how the principles learned in sessions 2-7 are working.

Couples are to prepare for this session by answering the following questions. Start your sessions with question 1 but after that let the group choose which question they would like to talk about.

1. Share your thoughts and feelings about your together times.

2. What examples of openness did you experience in your marriage this week?

3. What examples of acceptance (of accepting and being accepted) did you experience this week?

4. What is God doing in your marriage?

5. Is there something about marriage in general you would like to discuss?

6. Can you share an insight that has helped you this week?

7. What are you wrestling with? In what areas do you still need help?

(Eight is to be completed in private at the end of your group session and then with your spouse during the week).

8. Because of the insights of this session I will _____ .

Before Session 8 is over ask couples if they would like to get together in a month or so for fellowship and caring. Try to set the date while the group is together. Reunions can be a big boost to those who are committed to having a growing marriage.

Marriage Retreat or Seminar

A marriage retreat or seminar takes a bit more organization but, with the following plan it can be a simple, effective way to help other couples. This plan is for a weekend—Friday evening and Saturday. It can be a retreat setting or at the church.

I suggest that you use the same small-group approach that was explained for "Couple to Couples." There are two major differences.

First, you will need other lead couples if you have more than five couples attending. For training you could form a small group with your lead couples and go through the five sessions of the retreat. A shorter but less effective method would be to have lead couples read the book and have a meeting discussing some of the questions and overall organization of the retreat.

Second, couples will not have a week to prepare for the session. This can be handled by a "preparation time" prior to each session. Following is a way the weekend can be organized.

Session 1—Introduction
7:30-8:30 P.M. Friday

Start off with a large-group session explaining how the weekend will work. Give each couple a schedule and assign couples to their groups. Distribute the books.

Have couples go to their small groups for a get-acquainted time. Use some of the questions from Session 1 of the "Couple to Couples" section.

Preparation time for the next session: Explain to couples that the next session is at 9:00 A.M. Saturday morning and by that time they should have read step 1 and answered the corresponding questions.

Session 2—A Commitment to Growth in Our Marriage
9:00-10:00 A.M. Saturday

Have couples share in small groups. Use guidelines for Sessions 2-7 in "Couple to Couples" section.

Preparation for next session. Explain to couples that they will have until 1:00 P.M. to prepare for the next session. They are to read, step 2 "A Commitment to Have Weekly Together Times," have a together time, and then answer the questions at the end of the chapter.

Session 3—A Commitment to Have Weekly Together Times
1:00-2:00 P.M.

Have couples share in small groups. Use guidelines for Sessions 2-7 in "Couple to Couples" section.

Preparation for next session, step 3. "A Commitment to Be Open with Each Other." Tell couples that they have until 4:00 P.M. to read the chapter and answer the questions.

Session 4—A Commitment to Be Open with Each Other
4:00-5:00 P.M.

Have couples share in small groups. Use guidelines for Sessions 2-7 in "Couple to Couples" section.

Preparation for Session 5. For Session 5 have couples read step 5, "A Commitment to Accept My Spouse" and answer the corresponding questions. Couples have until 7:30 to complete this assignment.

Session 5—A Commitment to Accept My Spouse
7:30-8:30 P.M.

Have couples share in small groups. Use guidelines for Sessions 2-7 in "Couple to Couples" section.

There are many ways you can rearrange the schedule to fit your needs. For example, if you have a three-day retreat you could schedule more free time between sessions or expand the sessions to one-and-a-half hours each. The suggested seminar retreat plan allows you to determine the time and length of meals and amount of free time.

BIBLE SCHOOL ELECTIVE

Yet another way to help couples in your church is through Sunday School. An advantage to this time is that you do not have to take another night of the week. Two disadvantages are (1) you have less time for the sessions and (2) attendance is generally not consistent.

I suggest that you set up Sunday School electives the same basic way in which the "Couple to Couples" (small group) is organized. Have eight sessions with the couples doing the required reading and questions to prepare for each session. Limit the enrollment of each group to 10 persons including the lead couple. Ask for the same commitment that is suggested for small groups in the home.

WILL YOU PASS IT ON?

Pray about this. I believe great things can happen to families in our churches when persons like you will commit yourselves to pass on the important principles you are striving to live out in your own marriage. Will you pass it on?

Note
1. H. Norman Wright, *The Christian Faces . . . Emotions, Marriage, and Family Relationships* (Denver: Christian Marriage Enrichment, 1975).

52 good list of goals

44-45 too much emphasis on accepting self

49-50 great analogy for how you need to water memories

49 emphasis on "me"

42-3 stages of memories